T0083153

Canticles of Light

Bob Chilcott

for upper-voice choir, SATB choir, and orchestra

Vocal score

MUSIC DEPARTMENT

OXFORD
UNIVERSITY PRESS

OXFORD
UNIVERSITY PRESS

Great Clarendon Street, Oxford OX2 6DP, England
198 Madison Avenue, New York, NY10016, USA

Oxford University Press is a department of the University of Oxford.
It furthers the University's aim of excellence in research, scholarship,
and education by publishing worldwide

Oxford is a registered trade mark of Oxford University Press
in the UK and in certain other countries

© Oxford University Press 2000

The moral rights of the author have been asserted

Database right Oxford University Press (maker)

First published 2000

All rights reserved. No part of this publication may be reproduced,
stored in a retrieval system, or transmitted, in any form or by any means,
without the prior permission in writing of Oxford University Press,
or as expressly permitted by law. Enquiries concerning reproduction
outside the scope of the above should be sent to the Music Copyright
Department, Oxford University Press, at the address above

Permission to perform the work in public
(except in the course of divine worship) should normally be obtained
from the Performing Right Society Ltd. (PRS), 29/33 Berners Street,
London W1T 3AB, or its affiliated Societies in each country throughout
the world, unless the owner or the occupier of the premises
being used holds a licence from the Society

Permission to make a recording must be obtained in advance
from the Mechanical Copyright Protection Society Ltd. (MCPS),
Elgar House, 41 Streatham High Road, London SW16 1ER,
or its affiliated Societies in each country throughout the world

ISBN 978-0-19-343288-8

Music and text origination by
Barnes Music Engraving Ltd., East Sussex
Printed in Great Britain on acid-free paper by
Halstan & Co. Ltd., Amersham, Bucks.

English translations by George Chukinas © Oxford University Press 2000
Cover design by Philip Atkins

Canticles of Light is scored for upper-voice choir, SATB choir, 2 flutes, oboe, 2 clarinets in B flat, bassoon, 2 horns in F, tubular bells, timpani, and strings. If the requisite forces are not available, the wind and brass parts may be substituted with a reduction for organ, arranged by Antony Baldwin. All orchestral material, including the organ reduction, is available to hire from the publisher.

In addition, the accompaniment exists in a version for organ and tubular bells alone, prepared with the help of Sarah Baldock. This is available to purchase from the publisher, ISBN 0-19-335538-8.

Contents

1. Te lucis ante terminum 1
(Before the end of day)

2. Christe, qui, splendor et dies 7
(Christ, brightness of the light of day)

3. O nata lux de lumine 16
(O light born of the light)

Composer's note

Canticles of Light is a setting of three Latin Hymns from the *Liturgia Horarum*. The first two, which are dark in character, are evening hymns that entreat God for protection and comfort through the night. The music lightens for the final hymn, a song for the morning, which expresses the belief that, with God's help, the light of day will encourage new strength and hope.

Bob Chilcott

In performance, the upper-voice choir can be situated away from the mixed choir and orchestra, to give distance to the quasi-plainsong melodies that they sing.

Commissioned in the year 2000 by Winchester Music Club in celebration of the 75th Anniversary of its founding by Sir George Dyson

Canticles of Light

BOB CHILCOTT

1. *Te lucis ante terminum*

Hymn at Compline
from *Liturgia Horarum*

* Translation by George Chukinas © Oxford University Press 2000.

© Oxford University Press 2000

Printed in Great Britain

OXFORD UNIVERSITY PRESS, MUSIC DEPARTMENT, GREAT CLARENDON STREET, OXFORD OX2 6DP

Photocopying this copyright material is ILLEGAL.

creator of all things, we ask you . . .

20
mp cresc.
mf
ut so - li - ta cle - men - ti - a sis prae - sul ad cus - to - di -
pos-ci-mus, ut so - li - ta cle - men - ti - a sis prae - sul ad cus - to - di -
- mus, ut so - li - ta cle - men - ti - a sis prae - sul ad cus - to - di -
- tor, ut so - li - ta cle - men - ti - a sis prae - sul ad cus - to - di -
. . . with your wonted kindness be our protector and guardian.
25
UPPER-VOICE CHOIR
mp cantabile
Te cor - da nos - tra som-ni-ent,
p dolce
- am. Te cor - da nos - tra som - ni -
- am. Te cor - da nos - tra som - ni -
- am. Te cor - da nos - tra som - ni -
- am. Te cor - da nos - tra som - ni -
mf
p dolce
Let our hearts dream of you,

30
te per so-por - em sen - ti - ant, tu - am - que sem - per glo-ri-am
S.
A.
- ent, te per so - por - em sen - ti - ant, tu - am - que sem - per glo - ri -
T.
B.
let us feel you near while sleeping,
and let us celebrate always your eternal glory in the light of the new dawn.
34
vi - ci - na lu - ce con - ci - nant.
- am vi - ci - na lu - ce con - ci - nant.
mp dolce
38
BASSES
p
B.
Vi-tam sa - lu - brem tri - bu - e,
p poco marcato
Grant our bodies health,

42
S.
mp cresc.
A.
ta - e-tram noc - tis ca - li - gi-nem
T.
poco cresc.
nos-trum ca - lo - rem re - fi - ce,
B.
mp cresc.
poco cresc.
mp cresc.
restore our strength,
and let the foul gloom of the night . . .
46
mf cresc.
tu - a col-lus - tret cla - ri-tas.
mf cresc.
mf cresc.
p
. . . be illuminated by your brightness.
51
p espress.
S.
A.
Prae-sta, Pa - ter om - ni - po - tens,
per Je-sum Chris-tum Do-mi-
T.
Bar.
p espress.
Do all this, omnipotent Father,
through Jesus Christ the Lord . . .

57
S.
A.
T.
Bar.
mp cresc.
- num, qui te - cum in per - pe - tu-um reg - nat cum Sanc-to
(+ BASSES)
mp
. . . who reigns with you and the Holy Ghost forever.

62
UPPER-VOICE CHOIR
f
p dolce
Spi - ri - tu. A - men,
(BARITONES)
p

2. *Christe, qui, splendor et dies*

Hymn at Compline
from *Liturgia Horarum*

82
SOPRANOS
p espress.
S.
Chris-te, qui, splen-dor et di-es, noc-tis
p
Christ, brightness of the light of day, you who roll away the
86
mp
te-ne-bras de-te-gis, lu-cis - que lu-men cre-de-ris, lu-men be-a-tis
mp
shadows of the night, who bestowed the light of light, telling of the light to come for the blessed,
90
mf
prae-di-cans,
p espress.
Chris-te, qui,
A.
Chris-te, qui,
T.
qui,
B.
Chris-te, qui,
mf
p
Christ, brightness of the light of day,

you who roll away the shadows of the night,

who bestowed the light of light, *telling of the light to come for the blessed.*

101
mp espress.
105
S.
A.
T.
B.
mp
f
Pre - ca - mur, sanc - te Do - mi-ne, hac noc - te nos cus -
We pray, Holy Lord,
that you watch over us this night;
109
mf
mp
-to - di - as; sit no - bis in te re - qui - es, qui -
-to - di - as; sit no - bis, no - bis in te re - qui - es, qui -
let us find rest in you,
and grant

113
dim.
p
-e - tas ho - ras tri - bu - e.
dim.
p
-e - tas ho - ras tri - bu - e.
dim.
p
-e - tas ho - ras tri - bu - e.
dim.
p
-e - tas ho - ras tri - bu - e.
p espress.
us peaceful hours.
117
pp cresc.
Som - no si
pp cresc.
Som - no si dan - tur
pp cresc.
Som-no si dan - tur o-cu-li,
pp cresc.
Som - no si dan - tur o-cu -
Though our eyes be given over to sleep,

122
cresc.
mf
dan - tur o - cu - li, cor sem - per ad te vi - gi - let; tu -
o - cu - li, cor sem - per ad te vi - gi - let, ad te vi - gi - let, tu -
cor sem - per ad te vi - gi - let, cor sem - per ad te vi - gi - let; tu -
- li, cor sem - per ad te vi - gi - let, ad te vi - gi - let; tu -
Let our hearts be filled with you through the night;
and with

126
f
- a - que dex - tra pro - te - gas fi - de - les, qui te di - li - gunt.
your right hand protect the faithful who cherish you.

129
mf
cresc.
in - si - di - an - tes re - pri - me, gu - ber - na
in - si - di - an - tes re - pri - me, gu - ber - na
De - fen - sor nos - ter, as - pi - ce, gu - ber - na tu - os
De - fen - sor nos - ter, as - pi - ce, gu - ber - na tu - os
mf poco pesante
cresc.
f
Look upon us, our protector, check those who beset us, and guide your servants . . .
133
f
ff molto legato
tu - os fa - mu - los, quos san - gui - ne mer - ca - tus es. Sit, Chris - te,
tu - os fa - mu - los, quos san - gui - ne mer - ca - tus es. Sit, Chris - te,
fa - mu - los, quos san - gui - ne mer - ca - tus es. Sit, Chris - te,
fa - mu - los, quos san - gui - ne mer - ca - tus es. Sit, Chris - te,
ff legato
. . . whom you have redeemed with your blood.
Glory be to you Christ,

137
rex pi-is-si-me, ti - bi Pa - tri-que glo-ri-a, cum Spi - ri-tu Pa -
rex pi-is-si-me, ti - bi Pa - tri-que glo-ri-a, cum Spi - ri-tu Pa -
rex pi-is-si-me, ti - bi Pa - tri-que glo-ri-a, cum Spi - ri-tu Pa -
rex pi-is-si-me, ti - bi Pa - tri-que glo-ri-a, cum Spi - ri-tu Pa -
holiest of kings, and to the Father,
and to the Holy Ghost . . .
141
f
- ra - cli - to, in sem-pi-ter - na sae-cu-la,
- ra - cli - to, in sem-pi-ter - na sae-cu-la,
f
mf dim.
- ra - cli - to, in sem-pi-ter - na sae-cu-la, in
f
- ra - cli - to, in sem-pi-ter - na sae-cu-la,
mf
. . . forever and ever.

145
mp dim.
in sae-cu - la.
mp dim.
in sae-cu - la.
mp dim.
sae-cu-la,
in sae-cu - la.
mp dim.
in sae-cu - la.
mf dim.
mp dim.
149
p
mp
p
A - men, A - men, A - men, A -
A - men, A - men, A - men, A -
A - men, A - men, A - men, A -
A - men, A - men, A - men, A -
p espress.
mp

3. *O nata lux de lumine*

Hymn at Laudes

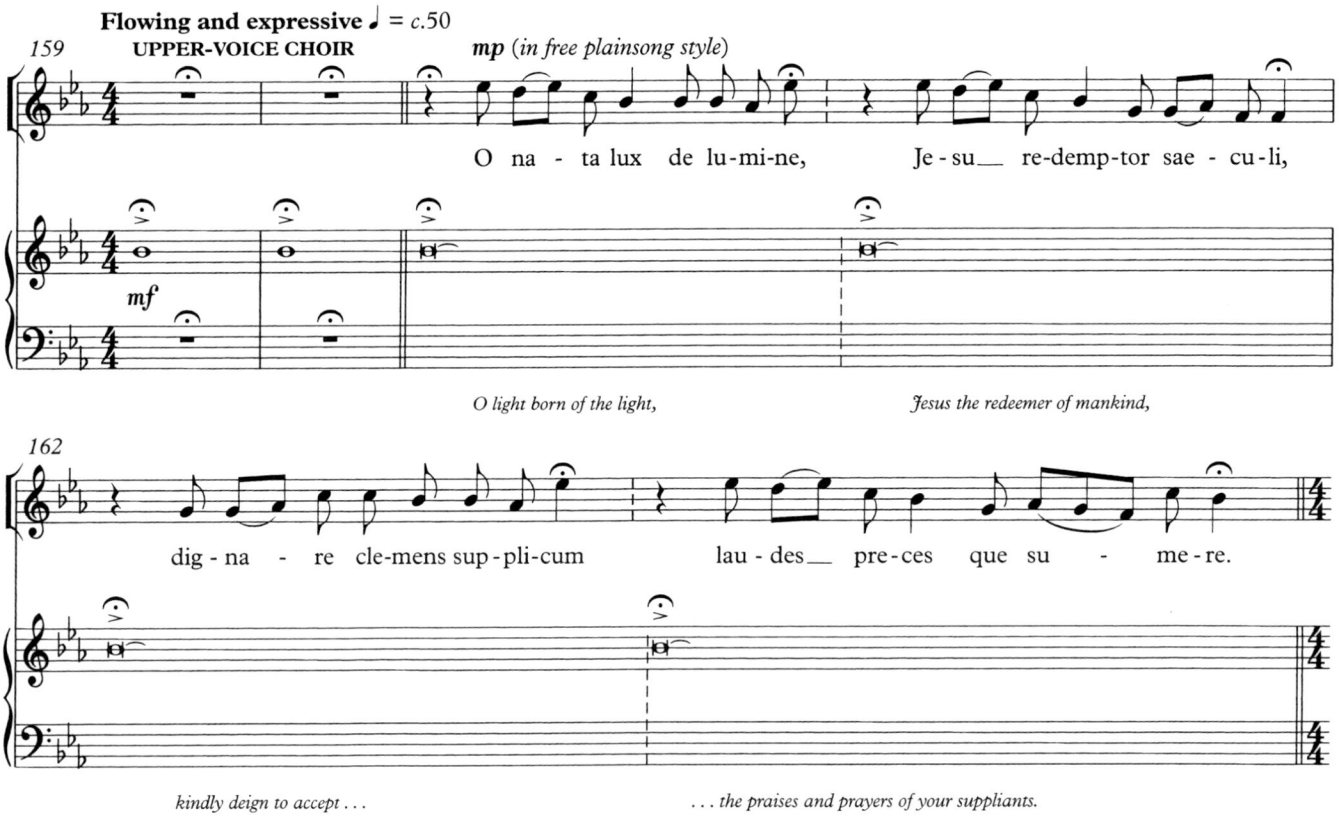

163
UPPER-VOICE CHOIR
mp espress. (in strict time)
O na - ta lux de lu-mi - ne, Je -
S.
p legato
O na - ta lux de lu - mi - ne, Je - su re -
A.
p legato
O na - ta lux de lu - mi - ne, Je - su re -
T.
p legato
O na - ta lux de lu - mi - ne, Je - su re -
B.
p legato
O na - ta lux de lu - mi - ne, Je - su re -
(Keyboard reduction)
mf
(Optional accompaniment)
p legato
O light born of the light,
Jesus the redeemer of mankind,
169
- su re - demp - tor sae - - cu - li, dig - na - re cle -
S.
A.
- demp - tor sae - cu - li, dig - na - re cle - mens sup - pli -
T.
B.
kindly deign to accept . . .

173
- mens sup - pli - cum lau - des pre-ces que su - me - re.
- cum lau - des pre - ces que su - me - re.
. . . the praises and prayers of your suppliants.

178
S.
A.
T.
B.
mf espress.
Qui car - ne
(Keyboard reduction)
poco cresc.
mf
You who once stooped

184
SOPRANOS
mf espress.
f
Qui car - ne quon-dam con - te - gi dig - na - tus es pro per - di -
ALTOS
mf espress.
f
Qui car - ne quon - dam con - te - gi dig - na - tus
f
quon-dam con - te - gi qui car - ne con - te - gi, dig - na - tus
BASSES
mf espress.
f
Qui car - ne quon-dam con - te - gi dig - na - tus es pro
cresc.
f
to take on human form . . .
. . . on behalf of those who were lost,
187
mf
mp
- tis. Nos mem-bra con - fer ef - fi - ci, tu - i be - a - ti
mf
mp
es pro per-di - tis. Nos mem-bra con - fer ef - fi - ci, tu - i be - a - ti
mf
mp
es pro per-di - tis. Nos mem-bra con - fer ef - fi - ci, tu - i be - a - ti
(BARITONES)
mf
mp
per-di - tis. Nos mem-bra con - fer ef - fi - ci, tu - i be - a - ti
mf
mp
grant that our weary limbs . . .
. . . find a resting place in you.

191
cor - por - is.
cor - por - is.
cor - por - is.
cor - por - is.
mf espress.
197
UPPER-VOICE CHOIR
mp (in free plainsong style)
O na - ta lux de lu-mi-ne, Je-su re-demp-tor sae - cu-li,
dim.
p
mf
O light born of the light, Jesus redeemer of mankind,
201
rit. e dim. al fine
dig-na - re cle-mens sup-pli-cum, lau-des pre-ces que su - me-re.
mp
p
kindly deign to accept . . . . . the praises and prayers of your suppliants.